Presented to:

Never Forget The Difference You've Made

[illegible]

[illegible]